This book belongs to

_____

_____

and I am finding out
about God

Copyright © 2016 Lion Hudson/Tim Dowley Associates Ltd
Illustrations copyright © 2016 Eira Reeves

The right of Eira Reeves to be identified as the illustrator of this
work has been asserted by her in accordance with the Copyright,
Designs and Patents Acts 1988.

All rights reserved. No part of this publication may be
reproduced or transmitted in any form or by any means,
electronic or mechanical, including photocopy, recording or any
information storage and retrieval system, without permission in
writing from the publisher.

Published by Candle Books
an imprint of
Lion Hudson plc
Wilkinson House, Jordan Hill Road,
Oxford OX2 8DR, England
www.lionhudson.com/candle

ISBN 978 1 78128 275 5
e-ISBN 978 1 78128 311 0

First edition 2016

A catalogue record for this book is available
from the British Library

Printed and bound in China,
April 2016, LH06

Would you like to know about God?

by Tim Dowley
Illustrated by Eira Reeves

CANDLE BOOKS

Who is God?

The Bible tells us about God.

It has stories about people long ago who believed in God.

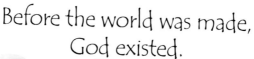

Before the world was made,
God existed.

God made the world.

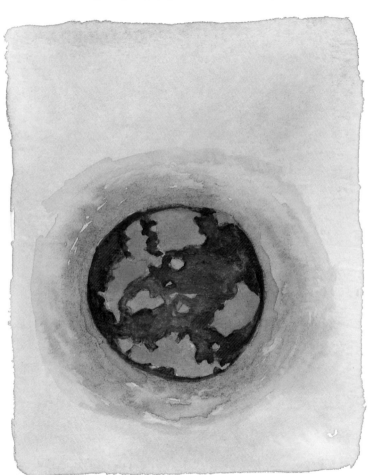

He made the sun, moon, and stars.

What does God look like?

No one knows!

But the Bible tells us a lot about him.

God is like a mother bird,
who looks after her chicks.

He is like a strong rock,
where we can be safe from danger.

What does God do?

God looks after our world.
He's in charge of the sun,
the wind, and the rain.

God knows about
everything that happens.

Even when bad things happen,
God takes care of us.

God is good.

God loves us.

And God forgives us.

God is close to us and helps us.

God cares for everyone

– especially those who have
no one else to help them.

Can we talk to God?

We speak to God when we pray.

We can be safe in his love forever.
God is for always.
He never changes!